I'm so sorry that you're here.

This grief journal is filled with lined pages. Each page is just for you to write down all those feelings and words that you don't feel able to share with anyone else right now.

It's OK to allow your emotions to fill the pages of this journal. That's what it's for.

There is no right way to use this journal. Simply do whatever works for you.

Made in the USA
Monee, IL
04 May 2022